NATIONAL MONUMENTS

NATIONAL MONUMENTS

Heid E. Erdrich

MICHIGAN STATE UNIVERSITY PRESS ▪ *East Lansing*

⊛ The paper used in this publication meets the minimum requirements
of ANSI/NISO Z39.48-1992 (R 1997) (Permanence of Paper).

 Michigan State University Press
East Lansing, Michigan 48823-5245

Printed and bound in the United States of America.

19 18 17 16 15 14 13 12 11   2 3 4 5 6 7 8 9 10

LIBRARY OF CONGRESS CATALOGING-IN-PUBLICATION DATA
Erdrich, Heid E. (Heid Ellen)
National monuments / Heid E. Erdrich.
p. cm. — (American Indian studies series)
ISBN 978-0-87013-848-5 (pbk. : alk. paper)
1. Indians of North America—Poetry. I. Title.
PS3555.R418N38 2009
811'.54—dc22
                               2008029585

Cover and book design by Sharp Des!gns, Inc., Lansing, Michigan
Cover artwork is *Vaster Empire* (2007) by Andrea Carlson and is used
with permission.

g green press Michigan State University Press is a member of the Green
INITIATIVE Press Initiative and is committed to developing and en-
couraging ecologically responsible publishing practices. For more infor-
mation about the Green Press Initiative and the use of recycled paper in
book publishing, please visit *www.greenpressinitiative.org*.

Visit Michigan State University Press on the World Wide Web at
www.msupress.msu.edu

*To those living who hold the dead in their hands,
to the dead who give their bodies to the living
—and the wisdom to know the difference.*

✳   ✳   ✳

Contents

Acknowledgments

Some of the poems in this collection were previously published, some-times in an earlier version: "Butter Maiden and Maize Girl Survive Death Leap," in *Sister Nations: Native American Women Writers on Commu-nity* (Minnesota Historical Society Press, 2002); "Ghost Keeper," in *Cold Mountain Review* (Fall 2005); "Ghost Prisoner," "Ghost of Love," "Ghost Town," and "Ghost Nation," in *Speakeasy,* no. 19 (2006); "Goodnight" in *Many Mountains Moving* 9 (2008); "Infinite Progression," in *Ninth Let-ter* (Fall/Winter 2006); "Liminal," "Gazing Globe," and "eBay Bones," in *Poetry International: To Topos* (2007); "The Lone Reader and Tonchee Fistfight in Pages," "Made in Toyland," and "Mahto Sapha, Bear Butte," in *Yellow Medicine Review* (Winter 2007).

Gratitude

Thanks to John Burke, my family, and my writing friends whose conver-sations initiated several poems here. Thanks to Anna Crosby and Ashley Hagman for care of our children.

A grant from the Minnesota State Arts Board allowed me to travel and read from this book in 2008. The Loft Literary Center in Minneapo-lis has been my church of choice for fifteen years and has my gratitude forever.

My particular thanks to fellow poet and editor Eric Gansworth, whose comments and expert knowledge of the bat cave greatly influenced this collection. To the staff of Michigan State University Press: *Mii gwetch*!

GRAVE MARKERS

National Monuments

Low house of rough bark,
small enough for a fairy
delights my sight

until it's clear it covers a grave
and worse, it's stained deck-red
shingled with asphalt.

Some park official has kept up
what was meant to moss
and rot and fall.

Grave houses, clan-marked:
sturgeon scratched in pine,
simple lines of eagle and marten,

whiskered totems, some on crosses.
Other tribes carve headstones:
Six-Nations' eel flips its infinity of tail ∞

Bear tracks tell complex genealogy,
map land and tongue and history
to crane's stick legs and turtle's shell.

Doodem signs, national markers
the body makes by being born,
that speak your only, only name,

your last word etched, kept, engraved.

Guidelines for the Treatment of Sacred Objects

If the objects emit music,
and are made of clay or turtle shell,
bathe them in mud at rainy season.
Allow to dry, then brush clean
using only red cloth or newspaper.
Play musical objects from time to time.
Avoid stereotypical tom-tom beat
and under no circumstances dance or sway.

If objects were worn as funerary ornament,
admire them verbally from time to time.
Brass bells should be called *shiny*
rather than *pretty.* Shell ear spools
should be remarked upon as *handsome,*
but beads of all kinds can be told,
simply, that they are *lookin' good.*

Guidelines for the treatment of sacred objects
composed of wood, hair (human or otherwise)
and/or horn, include: offering smoke,
water, pollen, cornmeal or, in some instances,
honey, chewing gum, tarpaper
and tax incentives.

If an object's use is obscure,
or of pleasing avian verisimilitude,
place rocks from its place of origin
within its display case. Blue-ish rocks
often bring about discovery, black rocks
soothe or mute, while white rocks irritate mildly.
All rocks must return to their place of origin

whenever they wish. Use only volunteer rocks,
or stones left by matri-descendant patri-tribalists.

Guidelines for the treatment of sacred objects
that appear or disappear at will
or that appear larger in rear view mirrors,
include calling in spiritual leaders such as librarians,
wellness-circuit speakers and financial aide officers.

If an object calls for its mother,
boil water and immediately swaddle it.
If an object calls for other family members,
or calls collect after midnight, refer to tribally
specific guidelines. Reverse charges.

If objects appear to be human bone,
make certain to have all visitors stroke
or touch fingertips to all tibia, fibula
and pelvis fragments. In the case of skulls,
call low into the ear or eyeholes, with words
lulling and kind.

If the bones seem to mock you
or if they vibrate or hiss,
make certain no mirrors hang nearby.
Never, at anytime, sing *Dem Bones.*

Avoid using bones as drumsticks
or paperweights, no matter
the actions of previous Directors or Vice
Directors of your institution.

If bones complain for weeks at a time,
roll about moaning, or leave chalky outlines,
return them instantly to their place of origin,
no questions asked. C.O.D.

Mahto Paha, Bear Butte

Her blueness,
her sleeping back,
curled to offer retreat,
respite from the dry land
surrounding for miles and miles.
Who wouldn't want to pray here?
Offer on the deep green pines and wind,
dream on this dreamer, share her vision—
Or rally up from the interstate on hawgs,
bullying noise like a second cavalry
bound for a biker's paradise.
Talk of tailpipes and chrome might drown
sacred words pines speak with wind—
But who wouldn't put their church here?
To gather and praise at Mahto Paha
cool in the shadow of her curled form,
tucked right under her yawning paw.

Black and White Monument, Photo Circa 1977

I

Everything that ever happened
lies outside the white border
of this photo taken in the late 1970s.

Two girls holding babies in strong light with a field in the distance.

The girls' faces, obscured in deep shadows
on the left, show the high planes of their faces
in bright relief on the right. Not a good shot.

Not one to put in an album or mount in a frame or ever look at again.

We only knew each other those few hours
before and after the shutter snapped.

We hauled those babies, offspring of older cousins,
all over our Grandpa's land that one reunion weekend
and then never saw one another again.

Who were those babies? Which of our many cousins?
The girl in my arms, sweet-faced and prettily dressed—
probably belonged to my grown up, glamorous cousin,
mother to three, already.

Our faces in half shade, strange above the babies' lit up scowls.

That cousin's baby, held against my relaxed arm,
my knee, beneath her, clutched in my right hand—
the only grown up part of me. My long thighbones
slim for just that year, then rounded like the rest of me.
My pony legs and long wings of bangs above a shoulder-length fall
that matches my cousin's, dates the era.

Dark and light divide the shot. The light is off. The light is everything.

My grandparent's land stretches beyond us, the real subject of the photo.
The light on that land, beyond beautiful, went into me so young
it became the color of all yearning, all rest to be hoped for,
the face of heaven. Everything.

    II
Dark slashed with too bright light.
                    Two girls holding babies at sunset near a field.

Beyond the white border of the photo:
a cabin of oak logs chinked with mud.
Old clothesline poles where swallows nest.
A burn barrel for trash. And one young tree, a basswood wide
enough to give deep shade to the drinkers,
meshed to lawn chairs—there for hours
before and after the photo.

They'll tall talk and fish iced beers from a galvanized tub.
When that ice melts, they'll fill it with iron-belt well water
that smells slightly of blood.

We drank from the pump in teams:
one cousin primes it, then cold, cold water gushes down the other's throat,
spills across the other's chest, so everyone walks away wet.

We will get up from that picture, hauling those babies.
We will get up on our long, adolescent legs
and move among the men who tease us for our baby love,
the sweaty infants clinging to our damp shirts,
our short shorts and snapping eyes do not stop their comments one bit.

Not a good shot. Not one I'd ever look at with that cousin saying:
"Look at us, we were so young . . ."

The boy baby wears little man clothes and plaid shoes tied up nicely.
He looks like he might head to the office, broker a deal, make a mint.
He looks like there's a plan for him. But *we know different,* as we said then.
We all *know different.*

Don't we always know more or less than what a photo can show?

The girls in that photo wear braces, their lips puff up and part
when they mean to hold them stern, mean to avoid the eyes of men.

Not even a year later, they'll give in and want love
from any boy who drives them down dirt roads
bordered by sunflowers, hay, green corn.

      III
Dark and light divide the shot.
                            The light is off. The light is everything.

To think beyond the white border of that photo makes a click
                          deep in the cartilage that guards my heart.
It unfixes something in me where memory fights facts
                        about the half of us who have so little time.

Those beyond the border who would too soon die sick,
                    or senselessly, or go unrecognizable
in a life both dark then slashed with too bright light.

Why do we bear the cruelty of photos—the way they suggest anything
                    can stop, any moment can be saved?

Everything beyond that border comes along with that image
                    and then more images and more and more.

We got up, chased the toddlers until every beer was drunk
                         and every drunk passed out.
We turned a hose on those sleeping it off under the basswood,
                    then hauled ass back to the cabin.

We found our Uncle working a hot pan
of dredged and fried delicacies from a yearling doe
                    that Uncle shot as he leaned out his car window.

                    No one took his picture then
               or in the next moment when we sat down laughing
         and ate the tender meats, the muscle that pumped her life,
                    the best, most vital parts of that deer.

Grand Portage

Here is the path my people walked
hauling immense trade canoes,
the semi-truck of centuries past.

Here between Great Lake and Great North,
earth curves visibly toward the artic ice
that now flows in places never open before.

Here guests can hear a natural history
of the beaver, gold standard for
a century of trade from isle to inland.

Here re-enactments and regalia
keep history current, preserve trappers'
ways, traders' wares, all the era conveys.

Here ghostly silver warehouses of bare wood,
a portage path eight and a half miles:
full of meaning, necessary, contested.

Here a National Monument arose by
Presidential declaration to urgently protect
Gitche Onigaming's place in time.

Here begins North and territories beyond,
where ice opens a passage that, a century past,
would have made this path unnecessary, unprotected.

There the true path, the mark, the monumental.

Desecrate

Entry Word: desecrate. Function: verb. Text: to treat (a sacred place or object) shamefully or with great disrespect <vandals *desecrated* the cemetery last night with graffiti>. *Near Antonyms*: bless, consecrate, dedicate, hallow, sanctify; honor, respect; cleanse, purify.

—Merriam Webster Online Thesaurus

Shave Santa Clause

Tear roses from the pale hands of saints.

Render Chocolate Jesus down to kisses.

Melt, thaw and absolve into a dew . . .

Bulldoze the Sistine Chapel

Rubble-pile the pyramids

Rake the olive trees of Gethsemane

Fire the Dalai Lama

Burn the Library of Congress

Salt the Peace Gardens

Flood New Orleans

Blow out the Eternal Flame

Wreck it all for everyone.

AMERICAN GHOSTS

Post-Barbarian

> And now what shall become of us without any barbarians?
> Those people were some kind of solution.
>   —Constantine P. Cavafy, "Waiting for the Barbarians" (1904)

Such things as dazzled me,
emerald brilliance, glitter of
costly canes wonderfully carved
with silver and gold—mean nothing
now I've left the gates.
Left off my threats and treating,
ceased my distant drums and leaping
out at civil folk in dark barrens where my
young sleep piled like squirrels or dogs
or any creature you chose to call us.
Now what? Now who?
You draw a zone that attracts, holds terror
in its grasp, sticks flies in a paper trap.
Those bodies glitter, too, void, wrapped with yours,
litter the sand with metal husks and insect noise.
We see it on your televised maps and understand
fear of them keeps the vote in hand, solves
all economic woes, turns the key to homelessness,
best-guesses global warming,
antidotes AIDS, fixes inside fights,
unravels the mystery of misogyny,
tells the world: it's them-not-me.

So, we know what has become of you, who needed us,
your *kind of solution*. But what was it we once solved?
What was the quandary? Who asked the question?

Some Elsie

And there she sits, Elsie, in American Lit.,
at the Community College or Harvard or the U.
The sleek New York TA reads how her family
"married with a dash of Indian Blood"
and thus escaped the fate of the "pure products"
Wm. Carlos Wms. saw go crazy.

Does she sit, terrified or transfixed?
Waiting for someone to turn, look at her and think,
There she is, that Elsie.
So what if she was hemmed all around with murder?
Or if a few of her relatives had screws loose?
She'd deny bathing in filth from Friday to Sunday.
What a girl does on the weekend,
come on now, that's her own affair.

She endures the comments about her body,
"the great ungainly hips and flopping breasts"
What if her ample chest had been her pride?
What if, at first, she flushed at the sound of
"voluptuous water" and took it as a compliment?

What if, at first she thought, *Ah, at last
a poem about someone I know.*
Imagining that she'd strain after deer, too,
if stuck in the suburbs passing pills.
But now, even knowing her hips,
somehow become, the TA says, *a text,*
doesn't help the sting when she thinks
there's some truth she'd like to express,
broken brain or not.

Ghost Prisoner

This prisoner and other "ghost detainees" were hidden largely to prevent
the International Committee of the Red Cross from monitoring their treat-
ment and conditions, officials said.

—"Rumsfeld Ordered Iraqi Suspect Held as 'Ghost' Prisoner,"
San Francisco Chronicle, June 17, 2004

The ghost prisoner, a murderer,
wishes he was invisible, sheer air,
already dead. His narrow bed
washes him away to dream escape
through holy gaps that open
in the grin of his small son.
Lost teeth offer him a freedom
so absurd he wakes and laughs.

No one hears the ghost prisoner.
Whether he groans or bears stoically
what instruments we've paid to play
this march toward a freedom so absurd
we wake and silently shake our heads.
We do not speak ill of the dead.

The ghost prisoner, still murderer,
wishes he was visible, fiery air,
rallying the dead. His narrow cell
just the place for prayer. Holy, holy,
a ghost's revenge pushed through gaps
in his own gashed mouth, a curse
so absurd, he wakes to its howl.

No one says his name, his crimes,
how many jolts it took to resurrect
him as betrayer of insurrection,
paying for freedom's ring.

We do not want to know what it took.
We'd rather not speak the dead ill.
We do not want to know what it took
to make him wish he were dead still.

Made in Toyland

It's a spaghetti pot, self-critique.
Tangled strands loop, bend
and come back on themselves.
How easily thoughts slip,
slide into a mess of other thoughts.
Take this playroom through such a lens:
most everything in it depends on work
done by women's hands worlds away
where ills and tears and injury
matter less than children's need for gifts
and our own need to give so abundantly.
Those with no play-world of their own,
give so much to children, thinking
kids need stuff or believing
bristle-sided blocks and trucks that talk
look fun and maybe they can play along,
be children for awhile.
What do the women
who mold this plastic, work the seams
and package all these toys think?
Do they allow their own form of cultural critique?
Americans, crazy for junk for their kids.
Or do they chopstick thoughts, lift mouthfuls,
slurp from masses of doubt toward clarity:
Joy, their work brings joy to girls and boys.
So when our children shriek and play and toss toys
away, we seize on their delight
before our pasta pot of thought wriggles:
Is that enough? It better well be.

Ball it all as on a fork, swallow it down—
Toyland, toil, joy. Follow only the thought,
watch out each strand's not rope,
watch out you don't choke.

Ghost Keeper

The keeping of a ghost lodge is a signal of peace and cancels all grudges
between parties.

—Alice Fletcher, 1882

Orphans and the aged feast at the Shadow Lodge
open to the needy and the one who lingers.
No person who holds a grudge,
no person who goes to war
or means another harm may enter
where the father of the fallen child
keeps vigil, keeps the ghost, all year.

Every day the food is set, but Ghost Keeper
must eat no meat scrapings. Nor can he leave.
He must not shake his blanket nor disturb
the air where his child lingers.
He must be as a ghost himself—
he must not butcher or crack bones
when he eats, nor take a weapon
nor hold his wife, nor pick up any child.

He must not lift the living children
who are the envy of their shadow sibling,
the kept-ghost who might draw them near.

When it ends, the months of mourning,
it ends for good.

The kept-one released, the gifts are given:
buffalo robes, quill work, woven sashes,
calico, pipes, tobacco, hatchets.

Four days of gifts: moccasins,
knives, leggings, bells, blankets,
reed weavings, bows, shawls,
Gifts for all and all attend the feast
of dried cherries and squash and pounded meat.

And the Ghost Keeper lifts each child,
gallops them about like a pony gone wild.

Infinite Progression

If the mixed blood is a tragic mirror for Euroamerica, giving back a disturbing reflection, then the Euroamerican in turn would seem to offer no reflection at all for the mixedblood who gazes back.

    —Louis Owens, *MixedBlood Messages: Literature, Film, Family, Place*

Like most girls, Elsie avoided the mirror.
It distorted her, brought out her flaws.
Her aunties always taunted her about her nose:
turtle-beaked, turned a bit, not *Indin*, but *India-Indian*.

Vampires lucked out on the reflection thing,
Elsie thought. She combed her hair a lot and primped
in window reflections that minimized imperfections
and lent her torso elongated proportion.

But she wouldn't send anyone back across the ocean.
Which ancestor would she let go? The one who lent her
her long second toe? Or the ancient one whose blood
made hers the universal donor, safe for all others?

In a restroom once, Elsie saw how one mirror
gives back another
and that one gives another back
until dozens reflect in one frame.
That, she thought, is me:

Connected in all directions,
a walking picture of infinity.

In Search of Jane's Grave

In memory of Jane, wife of Henry R. Schoolcraft, Esq., born at St. Mary's Falls, 1800; died at Dundas, May 22nd; 1842, in the arms of her sister, during a visit at the house of the rector of this church, while her husband was in England and her children at a distant school. She was the eldest daughter of John Johnston, Esq., and Susan, daughter of Waubojeeg, a celebrated war chief and civil ruler of the Odjibwa Tribe.

—inscription at Jane Johnston Schoolcraft's grave

Woman of the Sound the Stars Make Rushing through the Sky,
Bamewawagezhikaquay, her headstone should have said.
But her name splits, eclipsed by his,
her co-author and husband.
Jane, wife of, it reads,
followed by a sonnet,
tightly rhymed to fit lines
together to say she died *bland*
and sure of immortality:
She smiled to quit a world of tears.

If only the words left us were hers.
Literary Grandmother,
first Ojibwe, mixed-blood,
Native, First Nations, Indian writer.
Mother poetess.

True, her verse hurts like 1830.
She kept current, do not doubt it,
wrote no worse than Longfellow,
who took her mother's family stories
(as offered by her husband, Schoolcraft)
and Hiawatha-ed the heck out of them.

In a small town cemetery, I thought
I'd found you, our literary Sky Woman.
Someone re-created your grave,
The sonnet at least, minus your name,
but nearer to your girlhood home
where you were known and loved as
Woman of the Sound the Heavens Make.

Dear Jane, hushing pines along the lake
should have sung you rest eternally—
peaceful on the point, Michigan
beating blue and flecked,
rushing like stars to the shore.

Not Seeing Ground Zero in 2005

Iraq saw the birth of cities, epic verse, and codified religion; the lions guard-
ing the New York Public Library are esthetic descendants of the smashed
terracotta masterpieces of Baghdad.

—*Science Daily*

Fur hats are all the rage
on Manhattan's streets, and we,
freed from the Midwest semester's end
hop a plane to see, perhaps, a play
or art lavished out like culture here
where the sky fell, the earth opened.

What if my companion asks me to go?
What if she wishes to see Ground Zero?

Street vendors offer us fine distraction,
rabbit fluff gloves, good against urban winds.
We seek fur boots, laced up the calf, like
Attila the Hun would wear but sexier.

Hun-wear abounds on the still healing streets
still hung with flags every block, and a clear
relief we keep meeting when people say
Good to get back to normal . . .

Yet, tourists flock to the mass grave,
the place where everything changed.
I picture chain-link fence and roses, poems,
prayers, more flags. We hear objects left
go into a special collection of thousands.

Still, we do not go where everyone supposed we'd go.

Shops distract with fabulous treasures.
The 15,000 things lost in Baghdad's Iraq Museum,
looted and plundered since the first Gulf War
couldn't have more fascinated us
than 50% off in the ladies department.

We do our own pillaging and, weighed with goods,
blasted in the wind of urban canyons,
seek the transit up to the West Side.

That's when we sense the gap at our backs,
sense some huge absence down the avenue . . .

We turn, like women in myths who cannot resist.

Nothing is there. Nothing we notice.

The nothing that is something lies brilliantly still
surrounded by searchlights. Nothing visible in their glare.

Liminal

from Whitman

Try to imagine the elastic vision of a child
whose chalky gray sidewalk
and rusted swing-set meant the world.

The whole enchanting world in flakes
sifted from cheap metal chains, to dress
what little snow's left on a certain part of one day.

The scant brown grass at snow's retreat—
a lovely world of moss, a valley for the little people.
A world that was so good to bring back life

from the breathless blank winter of the prairie.
And the treasure the snow showed:
Maple leaf glassed in ice, perfectly green still.

Cat-eye marbles encrusting the sandbox like jewels.
At season's edge what we find matters most:
We get back what is lost in flux.

Hard lesson yet, for a girl who grew up
leaning in the doorway,
yearning for waves so far from any shore.

The Theft Outright

after Frost

We were the land's before we were.

Or the land was ours before you were a land.
Or this land was our land, it was not your land.

We were the land before we were people,
loamy roamers rising, so the stories go,
or formed of clay, spit into with breath reeking soul—

What's America, but the legend of Rock 'n' Roll?

Red rocks, blood clots bearing boys, blood sands
swimming being from women's hands, we originate,
originally, spontaneous as hemorrhage.

Un-possessing of what we still are possessed by,
possessed by what we now no more possess.

We were the land before we were people,
dreamy sunbeams where sun don't shine, so the stories go,
or pulled up a hole, clawing past ants and roots—

Dineh in documentaries scoff DNA evidence off.
They landed late, but canyons spoke them home.
Nomadic Turkish horse tribes they don't know.

What's America, but the legend of Stop 'n' Go?

Could be cousins, left on the land bridge,
contrary to popular belief, that was a two-way toll.
In any case we'd claim them, give them some place to stay.

Such as we were we gave most things outright
(the deed of the theft was many deeds and leases and claim stakes
and tenure disputes and moved plat markers stolen still today . . .)

We were the land before we were a people,
earthdivers, her darling mudpuppies, so the stories go,
or emerging, fully forming from flesh of earth—

The land, not the least vaguely, realizing in all four directions,
still storied, art-filled, fully enhanced.
Such as she is, such as she wills us to become.

Ghost Town

Originally established as Frog Point in 1871, the name was changed to Bell-mont in 1879. It is said it was destroyed by a flood in 1897, and the post office closed in 1909.

—Ghost Town USA's Guide to the Ghost Towns
of North Dakota, roostweb.com

The park on the marshy bank is all that's left.
A hundred years and the slow flood of the Red
comes again, washing North what little debris
seventy-five souls could leave in the few decades
Bellmont North Dakota sat at Frog's Point.

And who was Frog? Who lay buried there?
Or in the cottonwoods full of Cheyenne bones?
And Métis bison hunters, did they camp on those banks,
thinking it theirs, but uninhabitable and haunted?
Did they sing so as not to hear the bones who cried
for long-gone relatives driven from this home?

Why put Bellmont there, with no train,
too much rain and gnats that gnaw you raw?
Post arrived until 1909, but who picked up the mail?
And that last card, sent to that address, what could
it have said but *We miss you here, wish we were there.*
That's the kind of mail I've always read
on antique postcards of the era—*love to all,* dated.
Or maybe that last missive never met its mark,
maybe it returned to sender when postal service ended.
Or did it go where letters go when dead?

De'an

Dogs so long with us we forget
that wolves allowed as how
they might be tamed and sprang up
all over the globe, with all humans,
all at once, like a good idea.

So we tamed our own hearts.
Leashed them or sent them to camp's edge.
Even the shrinks once agreed, in dreams
our dogs are our deepest selves.

Ur Dog, a Siberian, dogged
the heels of nomads,
then turned south to Egypt
to keep Pharaoh safe.

Seemed strange, my mother sighed,
when finally we got a hound,
. . . a house without a dog.

Her world never knew
a yard un-dogged and thus
unlocked. Sudden intrusions
impossible where yappers yap.

Or maybe she objected
to empty armchairs,
rooms too quiet
without the beat
of tail thump or paw thud.

N'de, Ojibwe say, *my pet,*
which also suggests *ode,* that spot in the chest,
the part you point to when you pray,
or say with great feeling—great meaning,
meaning dog-love goes that deep.

Ghost of Love

Having seen the last of him
at some reunion, or wedding or funeral—
He'll be satisfyingly shrunken, not the bull-chested
cowboy you fell for, not a man big enough
to catch you if you fell again—if you leapt,
hard for love, fell stone in love.

Who will he be years later?
Stricken, simplified, almost anonymous.
On the street you never would even pick him out.
Not even a shudder if he passes. Nothing there,
no ghost of love.

Until he corners you in a circle of dancers,
drinkers, mourners. It's the music betrays you:
something he seduced you to so long ago.

And he'll talk, move his deep eyes,
wanting to see if you still suffer, to see your old love,
to wake it up with a kiss and a charm—
make it his again.

He'll prod it until the hurt of years, accreted
around that old stone of love, rolls in you.
When he utters the word *forgiveness*

You'll open your mouth—a boulder will fall right out,
a concretion of old pain whose pit is love.
You'll know he's in its path and will be crushed,
but you will speak, you'll speak your rock.

Elsie Drops Off the Dry Cleaning

What's this in his pocket? A prescription pad.
If only she were bad, she'd write some 'ludes,
but instead she thinks to pen a few lines,
like the master himself, confine her desires
to the square under his name and Rx.

In the time it takes the rack to rotate,
her order's in, starch the white coats,
press the slacks for pick up in two days.
Meanwhile her mind's a hummingbird,
flits words to square, then darts away.
She needs more room, more lines.

Next store over's office supplies:
Big Chief tablets thick with lines,
the pulpy paper almost moist, acrid,
so soft pencil rips it. She buys crayon instead.

This is how Elsie winds up in American Lit.
First her words on Big Chief then, in years,
Son of Big Chief tablets appear. Her career
as a house-girl is long over. She hitchhikes:

Oklahoma, Colorado, South Dakota, takes lovers.
But her braids-n-shades warrior, without feathers,
whose beads and groovy vest protect her words,
does more for her than one man ever could.

Son of Big, as renewable as wood, dependable.
Tablets get her through the 70s drug-free,
nearly sober, raising kids and hell for AIM.
Then one day she enrolls in college, reads.

And writes, and writes, straddles a canon, makes a name.

Butter Maiden and Maize Girl
Survive Death Leap

Even now, Native American Barbie gets only so many roles:
Indian Princess, Pocahontas, or, in these parts, Winona—
maiden who leapt for brave love from the rock where eagles mate.

In my day, she might have played Minnehaha, laughing waters,
or the lovely one in the corn oil ads: "We call it maize . . ."
Or even Captain Hook's strangely erotic Tiger Lily.

Oh, what I would have done for a Chippewa Barbie.
My mother refused to buy tourist souvenir princesses
in brown felt dresses belted with beads, stamped Made in China.

"They're stunted," Mom would say. Her lips in that line
that meant she'd said the last word. She was right, those dolls
were stubby as toddlers, though they wore women's clothes.

Most confusing was the feather that sprouted at the crown
of each doll's braided hair. "Do they grow there?"
a playmate once asked, showing me her doll from Mount Rushmore.

I recall she gazed at my own brown locks then stated,
"Your mother was an Indian Princess." My denial came in an instant.
My mother had warned me: "Tell them that our tribe didn't have any
   royalty."

But there was a problem of believability, you see, a crumb of fact
in the fantasy. Turns out, Mom had floated in the town parade
in feathers, raven wig and braids, when crowned the college "Maiden."

Her escort was the college "Brave" they chose each autumn.
Oh, Mom . . . you made it hard on us, what you did at 18—
and worse, the local rumor that it was *you* on the butter box!

You on their toast each morning, you the object of the joke,
the trick boys learned of folding the fawn-like Butter Maiden's
naked knees up to her chest to make a pair of breasts!

I cannot count the times I argued for Mom's humble status.
How many times I insisted she was no princess, though a beauty
who just happened to have played along in woodland drag one day.

I wonder, did my sisters have to answer for the princess? Did you?
Couldn't we all have used a real doll, a round, brown, or freckled,
jeans and shawl-wearing pow-wow teen queen? A life-like Native Barbie—
better yet, two who take the plunge off lover's leap in tandem and survive.

The Lone Reader and Tonchee Fistfight in Pages

Have I not been your faithful sidekick?
Have I not been your faithful Indian guide?
Have I been, at least, your Sacajawea,
hankering for her mother tongue, slogging,
baby on the back and all? Your insider
reading the trail, trailing the readings
so as to point a way? Forgive me,
Kein No Sabe. You know not what
you know not, I know.
I do not mean to keep from you
tribal secrets, tribal sec-texts,
secret tribes or textual innuendo.
Only, my tongue refuses to fork, fork you
off into the path not-to-be-taken—
for that has made all our differences.

Ghost Nation

Birds burn upwards,
the sky falls.

Skies have fallen many times:
in the libraries afire,
the aviaries aflame,
parrots screaming their names,
streaks above Tenochtitlán.

The Ghost Nation grows,
swelled by thousands in one day.
The day the earth shook Turkey,
China, India, Japan.

Birds burn above New York's
perfectly blue sky.
Children mark their startled flights.
If they see dark figures fall,
plummeting as long ago heaven-cast,
they do not at first say, can not.

All in an instant, every instant,
comes a Ghost Nation.
Dark figures fall for the camera.
Names, ranked by floor, an assembly.

Birds burn upwards,
the sky falls. The sky fills.
Ghost Nation moves, moves as one.
More than enough to repeat us,
keep infants filled with souls.

Ghost Nation moves, moves as one
strong enough to keep the planet filled
to repeat its circle path.

White Noise Machine

Tuned to ocean waves
       soothing, and soothing and—
annoying gull shriek.

Beyond the sea sounds
       another whir and woosh
and gentle click, grunt.

Whir and woosh in a loop
       better to content any mother
than frog peep, or heartbeat.

Quickly there arises and flows
       around her the knowledge
and contentment that surpasses
       all other: her son's playing Legos.

No noise, but whir and woosh,
       gentle click of Weapons of Mini Destruction
coming into creation.

Star Blanket Stories

Shine in satin diamonds, eight pointed
worked in four colored fabrics, give-away gifts.

Good Girl, *nin Daanis,* comfort in these
baby blankets decorating your wall, now
you grow too tall to cover up with stars.

Soon you will be that young woman
sewing with her grandmother, bored,
noticing that one star twinkling right at you.

Tell your grandma, who will say,
"Pay no attention to that flashy boy!"

Wrap up tightly, when you go out at night
under his seductive light. Meet your Star Boy.

He'll ask you to run away
to bright lights, big solar systems.

Good Girl, say you have to ask.
Grandma will say "Are you kidding me? No, way!"

Once you go that path, breathe their blue air,
you can never come back.

Good Girl, tell your Star Boy
"I cannot leave my Kookums."

He'll say he'll wait for you.
If he doesn't, ditch him.

Star Boys have all the time in the world,
millions of minutes lit up on their cells
and light years to spark.

Each night he'll twinkle as you sew in the dusk.
For a while, that will be enough for you both.

But love means touch. And his is hot.
Finally, longing gets the best of you,
you give in and call him down.

Star Boy comes with an offering,
a neat logo design, free, in open use.

He says to Grandma, "She'll visit each morning."
East with the sunrise, our promise, that's you.

The people will make your image in praise—
Morning Star blankets, then quilts to give away.

You have two: one for birth, one for weaning.
Surely you'll get one to graduate, one to marry—
but no, that's right, you'll elope.

There's a reason they tell this story
absent the mother. Better Grandma bear it.

Astronomically distant from you, pretending
you still greet us each morning,
your face a blaze, nothing changed.

Do You Know the Secret of Johnnie's Cole Slaw Mix?

My pregnant sister asks across the plains full of
migrating geese and swollen rivers. Do I know?

EDTA to preserve freshness, could it be?
Or dehydrated, defatted, cream, sour cream and/or buttermilk?

Perhaps the secret lies in piles and piles of shredded nappa,
half a mango, three jalapenos and fresh cilantro to taste.
But no, not likely ingredients so far out on the prairie.

I do not know these Johnnies, or s/he may be only one,
variantly spelt, and full of arcane knowledge of the cabbage.
I do not know this cole slaw, though methinks I should . . .

The secret, do I know the secret? Ah ha! I believe I do.
What makes Johnnie's Cole Slaw Mix so good
happened months ago and will happen months hence.

The prize ingredient's a bun—you've just got to try one,
they make everything taste so much better, like butter.

Full Bodied Semi-Sestina

We take on pounds, heavy as cast iron,
We increase. We grow substantial, fat
even, and luxurious, although we tire
easily, puff in effort, purr and doze. We join
weight loss groups and confess and lift
up wafers of diet bread, punish our tongues.

What good is the human tongue
if it cannot lap molasses rich with iron,
fortification against poor blood? What a lift
we get from a little dab, some mono-fat,
mayo, or other loveliness. Won't you join
us in our lust, our great inflation of the spare tire?

It is not just about what we crave or that we easily tire
of ordinary fare. It's just we've lit the tongue
on fire. An urgent flame that leaps the join
between brain and body, makes food knowledge, iron-
hard fact to be visited, an experience. In command, Fat,
takes on her own life, though she's our burden to lift.

Or it may be she's simply unfit, no matter if fashion lifts
restrictive notions of where women can jiggle. Fad may tire
of the diamond between the thighs, impossible for body fat
in the normal range, not to mention genetics, the iron-clad
code we obey without knowing. A grandfather's love of tongue
sandwiches and sausage and schnapps is a club you join

just by being born. How simple is it to un-join?
How much must you want to lift
your own children from the shackles, the iron
set to weigh them down? Who wouldn't tire

with so much to bear? What prayer can we tongue
to deliver us all from fat?

It is not even that we hate our fat.
We love ourselves. We who join
the matrimony of flesh. To hold our tongues
begins a long divorce. Forks un-lift,
we deflate like a blown tire,
shouldered off-road tire-iron

in hand to beat the fat. *Iron
will!* Too tired a chorus to join,
yet we lift our tongues.

DISCOVERY—AN RSS FEED SERIES

Body Works

She labors. She efforts.
Raw as mutton, she functions.
Beloved body. Never leave me.

Never lend museums
your tissues, triceps, glutes.
Do not expose your inner works

as some corpse did,
in a busy airport
where a gray curtain gap

showed me jerked
and plasticized muscle
as my walkway glided past.

Work, just work.
Grin a death's head beneath
my plump and living cheeks,

but never leave me, body.
I will not make you art.

Even now she pumps, spasms,
pulps my dinner within her.
She works. Her blue fluids

meaningless and messy
illustrate nothing of her fine
compunction, her systole

and distally. She does it all
free and out of love for me.
Or so it seems.

She works. She labors.
My children, made in her,
came waxy and bloody enough.

Why would I want to know
any other innards than hers?
What intimacy has she spared

that I'd find splayed,
preserved and presented
upon a platform with expert didactics.

Work, just work. Make love.
What better act could she
perform in plastic?

Never leave me, body.
Though there's just one of me
and uncounted insatiable others

lined up to get a look
at what I take for granted:
guts, gonads, gallbladder,

your brilliant splash and gulp
hot hemoglobin,
vibrant hum of human synapse,

electricity that, if we listen
closely sings in any body.
Any body, believe me.

Bodies work.
We're proof enough.
Or we should be.

eBay Bones

Her skull goes to the highest bidder.
How much would you give for a warrior head?
Hawaii's history for an ashtray?
She was not much older than me.
Woman of volcanic earth so rich she probably
eased into the loam like her shawl,
wrapped up warm for her final sleep.
They should have buried her more deeply.
Should have thought of science's creepy needs.
Should have known the web would one day
hold our dead in its sacred sites.
The grave may be a fine and secret place,
but kept a fine secret only for some.
Others are History. And History
must be brought to light—
in the flash of an empty eye socket.

Someone will pay for this.
Someone did.
Her ivory grin worth
less than human curiosity,
less than the rest of all humanity,
all humanity at rest
beneath us all.

My Beloved Is Mine

A carbon-dated fossil called Toumai, [is] believed by many scientists to be the oldest known human. Others, however, dismiss Toumai as an ape.
—*Discovery News,* May 17, 2006

My love and I, in your *long-ago,*
side by side on the sea-beaten isle—
Me, her Zeus—her Jove, her Caliban, too.

Her kind hands, her pink-tipped touch,
speckled lips, lined and expressing nothing
but love and urgency. *The heart wants,*
what the heart wants. . . .

But let me say at once, we never
shared ancestors or parted ways,
to chart separate descendants,
split our differences.

And though she was no hobbit,
as some have called her, she was small.
Small, round-headed Toumai.
She loved me—that I know.
H. sapiens I whispered, *H. floresiensis*

We went everywhere together.
Gathered lusciousness the island afforded,
and clung together nights when
she grew helpless in her wild heat and
I could not help but be a man and
give her some relief.

Yes, we had our tender moments, we
bred and brought forth young
as quick and brown-eyed as lemurs.

Mooncalves and freckled whelps,
they frightened Toumai at times,
their greedy love of mother,
their ravishing humanity.

Huge so soon, they tumbled
her from time to time,
tugged her tufts of fur,
and teased her when they grew clever.

So it is we fed among the lilies,
while I peopled the island
with our race, all born of Toumai.

How it pains me to hear
you've carbon-dated her,
your oldest known human, your Eve.

Once, she was everything to me.
Brown and warm and womanly.
She elevated me, made me my best, made me a man.
Me, her Adam, her husband, her Caliban, too.

Ghostly Arms

The ghostly spiral arms of galaxy M106 were first detected in radio waves, contain no stars, and do not match up with the curved starry arms of the galaxy as seen by telescopes in visible light.

—Discovery News, April 19, 2007

We never know the moment
we end it.

An embrace spent,
time slips between
the moment lovers
let go,
and find it over.

Arms across the universe reach
and grasp at nothing
but the emptiness of space.

We never know the moment
we end it.

How warm were my arms
the last time I meant it
when I nested you in them?

How ghostly and misaligned
our caress would be
if we held each other now.

We never know the moment
we end it.

There comes an hour
And it is over. Forever,
the telescope of time tells us.

Creation itself fills with shadow arms
spinning in continual miss-match.
It is only at great distance

we ever know the moment
we end it.

Kennewick Man Tells All

We didn't go digging for this man. He fell out—he was actually a volunteer.
I think it would be wrong to stick him back in the ground without waiting
to hear the story he has to tell.
   —forensic anthropologist James Chatters in the *New Yorker,* June 16, 1997

Ladies and Gentleman of the press—

Kennewick Man will now make a brief statement
after which he will answer questions as time permits.

I am 9,200 years old

I am bone. I am alone.

Kennewick Man Swims Laps

For more than 40 years, the bones of about 12,000 Native Americans have
been kept in drawers and cabinets under the swimming pool of the Hearst
Gymnasium, next door to the museum.
                        —"Berkeley Accused of Racism over Failure to Return Tribal
                                    Bones," *Los Angeles Times*, February 27, 2008

Aquamarine with navy lines to keep
me in my lane. Lap, lap, lap
again and again until I hear
their watery voices beneath
repeating all I said when dead:

Peace, peace, peace and sleep.

A few cry out: *Remember me!*
But I am older than prayer,
and remember only river talk.

Lap, lap, lap, then turn in aqua *agua.*
I'm used to water, lay dead along
a river's edge nine millennia.

But water here's unnatural, vivid.
Still, I am older than religion,
—gotta keep limber. Lap, lap.

Aqua's such an off color,
new to me like rubber, milk,
electricity and jealousy.

Tribes and pre-Christian Folk groups
claim my water-logged bones as their own.
So too, the dead under lane seven. Lap.

May Day the Morris Dancers, subversive
at sunrise along chilly urban river banks,
shake bells and batons and ribbon bands . . .

Perhaps my kind?
Lap. Turn.
There is no mine.

I am older than any name for God,
swimming in the voices of blue-green ghosts,
in a place where color speaks

the way pool water changes shades,
renames itself with every ripple, every wave.

Kennewick Man Attempts Cyber-date

And then, one evening, I turned on the TV and there was Patrick Stewart—
Captain Picard of Star Trek, and I said, "My God, there he is! Kennewick
Man!"
    —forensic anthropologist James Chatters in the *New Yorker,* June 16, 1997

So when Cyber-date asks me what I look like,
I'm no liar.

Not like I expect to match a hottie.
Not looking for "Barbie and Kennewick Man"—

But to smell a woman's neck again!

Or just fill all required fields.
To simply state:
My age
My race
My God.

Prisoner No. 280

The Widow Capet,
buried in a mass grave,
quick-limed with her kind
and ignoble others, found
anonymity until her garter
gave her remains away
and they dug her up,
placed her by her husband's side
in the crypt for royal tenants.

There St. Denis stands with mitered head
in hand, his halo still aglow above
his raggedly chopped neck.

Saints before the time of guillotine
bore less scientific execution,
endured rough decapitations, yet walked,
some for miles. Their sermons they gave
to the last, to the grave made on the spot
where their bodies finally dropped.

Basilicas sprang up where such saints stopped,
churches fit for kings, their widows, and orphans,
who may have lost their heads, but none their hearts
—customarily embalmed as souvenir.

Prisoner No. 280 had given birth in public,
so execution merely brushed her dignity—
her last words a *pardon moi* as she tread
the executioner's boot.

The final words she left her boy asked
he not avenge her death. He lived eight years,
most in prison torture, forced drunkenness,
t.b., then death found the Lost Dauphin.

She would have died to save him,
and tried, when the military arrived to pry
the child from his mother. That's what it took.

His heart did survive, not embalmed,
but bottled by the surgeon in alcohol
until the days of testing DNA—
Marie's own mother mitochondria
identified the boy's heart as of the royal line.

In the year of her Lord, 2004,
they put that pickled organ to rest
with all the rest of the royals at St. Denis,
guarded by the headless patron of headache,
to whom we might now pray with all our hearts.

Vial

Recently, contact with the outside world has brought the Karitiana access to the Internet, where they discovered that their blood and DNA samples are being sold online.

—Lalo de Almeida for the *New York Times*

Tube of red
like a lipstick
passion's paint,
paid for, yet
unpaid for,
filched like a drugstore
compact pinched

Glass finger
slender vial of DNA
For Sale
to non-profits
yet non-bought
non-paid for.

Promised medicine,
Karitiana, Amazonian
indigenous, offered
blood and got
nothing

Rich and red
blood of hunger
bled in fear of

the next world wanting
the body whole,
each drop accounted for. . . .

When they sell it all,
they'll come back
for more.

Girl of Lightning

The bodies seemed so much like sleeping children that working with them felt "almost more like a kidnapping than archaeological work," Dr. Miremont said.

—*New York Times*, September 11, 2007

Thunder loves you,
mumbles charms to warm
you—folded cold body.

Lightning's pity picks you,
licks a kiss, but what's left
to wick?

Even direct hits miss—
no amount of flash and hiss
fires you. Inviolate virgin,

inflammable channel to Gods
long gone or gone underground,
ghost-gray flecks left in the rock

altar, your shelter for five centuries
where you huddled, red-painted
hair and wreathed with feathers.

Weave threads of your shawl—
not a shroud since you were live
when left for dead—weave cover

please, I beg your handlers.
Pull stitches so that wound closes
over your smoldered remains.

They say you clutch your mother's hair,
strands in a bag sent up the mountain,
an introduction to the Gods

of Science, who read threaded
DNA to determine who you
were related to when human.

Not the crushed boy near you,
no brother he nor sister the girl,
bound away to sacred silence,

cased in plastic cased in glass.
Visitors point and justify the past:
See what they did—child sacrifice.

Fattened 'em up, drugged 'em—
Spanish violence, Christian influence,
border fences, all deserved because of her

wad of coca leaves and elaborate braids.
Lightning's mark spares you display.
Singed cheek and blasted chest,

blackened flesh looks less asleep,
flashes back the fact you're dead,
a charred mummy, so far gone even

Lightning's longing couldn't wake you.
Thunder won't forget you, hums
a generator's song in cooler vents

to your coiled form in cold storage—
song of your six years plus five centuries
come to this: doom, doom, doom.

Lightning still sighs: *release, release, release.*

We Would Not Believe

"We open the Internet everyday, and the most important source you have are my spies," Hawass said. "I have spies all over the world, and those spies, they inform me every day of things you would not believe."

—*Discovery News,* April 10, 2007

Had Hawass said *imagine,*
we would have had him.

Imagine all creation taking place
in cyber-space. All beauty,
perversity, vast ennui
drifting like cosmic dust
along lines of light.

Just the other night we found
caterpillars can be identified
with the click of some keys.
Sticky? Spiky? Stripy?

All linked categories and also
names my children tried
until we found their catch called
Tent Worm, unfortunately.

We would not believe—
A mouse can make a weasel
tame as gerbils. Nocturnal, mink
hunch when they run, muskrat's
their favorite snack, and they
den under urban porches
until someone smells the pelts.

Then what? Google "mink control"
taking care to filter results
for filthy frisking females,
rarely males, perhaps a blessing.

We read and see, bathed, like saints
in halo, in attitudes of what
looks like belief.

Do *imagine,* searching images.
To believe, must jump the fault,
the divide in humanity, that trades skulls
and sneakers all at once.

Nefertiti's Close Up

Nefertiti, one of the ancient world's legendary beauties, may have had
wrinkles and bags under her eyes, according to a new investigation into the
famous bust bearing her likeness.

—Discovery News, September 5, 2005

Was not I The Great Royal Wife?
My renegade pharaoh called me *whom he loves.*
We overthrew the pantheon, raised the *Aten,*
then worshipped the Sun alone.

So the Sun touched me, drew my lips
to his and kissed until I flamed.
How hot His tongue, like the flick of a lizard.
So what if I bear His marks, His flecks and lines?

I know what historians say: Nefertiti vanished until
the bust found—found me radiant eternally.
The pedestal spot brought the Sun upon me again.
Again He spoke my true name: *The Beauty Arrived.*

Now the myth's destroyed, my iconic youth despoiled
by good lighting in an Italian museum study.
A mere man, Francesco Tiradritti, calls me a
"fascinating woman in her mature beauty."

What that does to me! Three thousand years
I went unwrinkled, mysterious, then under low light
in dark arrangements like an aging starlet.
Now museums urge, *use full lighting.* Like a make-over reveal . . .

If that scholar ever leans close, brushes my cheek again,
the way he caressed me in Berlin, I will not speak,
even if he knows my names, *Mistress of Sweetness,*
Lady of Two Lands, The Great Favour . . .

I'll stay still as sculpture, blank-eyed as history.
Age and beauty taught me one thing, Ladies:
Let no one less than a heavenly body possess you,
Oh, yes, make that your last and lasting gift, your love.

Pharaoh's Hair Returns

Locks of 3,200-year-old hair from the pharaoh Ramses II were unveiled at
the Egyptian Museum on Tuesday, returned to Egypt after being stolen 30
years ago in France and put up for sale on the Internet.

—*Discovery News*, April 10, 2007

Perhaps postal carriers in France make a pittance,
His only inheritance bandages and the hair of a pharaoh,
Ramses, whose works we look upon and delight.

Or mighty as we are, we might well tremble.
A hank of brown stuff over 3,000 years old,
like a web of mold that blooms under snow.

Who beholds such things without despair?
Yet, dead human hair's no different from our own.
So human hankering overrides horror for wonder.

How did the Internet auction go?
Up for Sale: Tufts of Pharaoh's Hair.
You are bidding on AAA+++ Real Human Remains.
Verified 100% curse-free and aged at least
three millennia. $2,600. Pay Pal only.
Serious bidders please, no Feds.

When bidding ends we have a winner,
Egypt gets the tresses back
and finally the curse is enacted:
the postman's punished. All's right,
unless you are the dead, still dead
and minus various pilfered parts.

Love your own body every moment.
It is only yours a while, then no longer
sovereign, if of interest to science,
or souvenir seekers or other, as yet
unspecified, future uses.

Antigone Finds the Field Grown Full

Where at first only her brother lies unburied,
lies alone, reddening in the sand and sun,
others come and her duty grows less clear.

What's owed this lot? Antigone wonders,
watching CNN, crouched beneath her black wrap,
waiting, crunching sand beneath her nails.

Her nightly scrambles past sentries,
her handful of dust defying the decree
he be left for crows—She'd do it for love,

but for a crowd? Who left them out?
Whose law or code? It all seems so very odd:
First, James Brown in sleek jacket, his pomp of hair

so shellacked the wind waves around his head,
leaves little runnels like halos, which suits his
preacherly air. Widows weep quite near.

She hears more than one, but none comes
to give him decent rites. Alone with the dead,
nights, she learns their names. The woman's
Anna. She's a sad one.

Her body marred with stitches, her hair
unbraided, her baby un-mothered, all undone.
Antigone goes to her after a time, offers sand,

fine, white mist drifts over the blown beauty.
When they come for this one she will slay them.
No one deserves her fate. Even the next corpse,

which appears to lie in state, is shrouded in dignity.
Indignity powers Antigone. Sentries damned,
she shovels night after night, lays even Christ to rest again.

When finally she's caught, they sentence her and her groom.
They marry in the tomb and sink deeply into each other.
No dozing off to TV news, they vow, and sleep together forever.

Personality

In the movie of my life
No one could play my mother.

Ann Miller wasn't Indian
and brunette beauties of a certain age
have all-but faded from the stage.

There are roles no one can fill
in the movie of my life.

But, in the movie of my life,
my husband could easily be played
by a young William Hurt, a benign
John Malkovich, or Max Headroom.

My three best friends
could cast themselves,
or accept a trio of Kates,
Caits, and Kathrines.

In the movie of my life
my Iroquois artist friend
rates Johnny Depp at least.

In the movie of my life
No one will be played by Adam Beach.

Jonis must be played by Bonnie Rait
whether Bonnie can act or not.

Melissa will be played by Halle Berry
crossed with the cuteness of Ugly Betty.
Halle Betty.

In the movie of my life
there are roles no one can fill.

The dead get cameos by icons.

In the movie of my life
My sisters would be played by
doe-eyed Canadian unknowns.

My brothers could all be cast
with members from the first two
troupes of Saturday Night Live.

In the movie of my life,
There are still two roles no one can fill:
my daughter and my son.

There will be no child actors
hell-bent toward tragedy
in the movie of my life.

In the movie of my life
there's just one role no one can fill,
since my generation lacks
the one recognizable zaftig actress.

In the movie of my life
I will just have to play myself.
Though my talent lags,
who else could I cast?

She Was the Kind

She was the kind
To tell it like it is
To kiss and tell
To kiss and kill
To kill with kindness

She was the kind
To get things through her thick skull
To work her fingers to the bone
To work on her back
To never take it lying down

She was the kind
To lay down the law
To get down on her knees
To get up on her feet
To give an inch and take a mile

She was the kind
To stand up for herself
To sit down strike
To go to the wall
To take it to the limit

She was the kind
To take it too far
To drop off the face of the earth
To face the music
To hit rock bottom

She was the kind
To get back on that horse and ride it
To get up on her high horse
To get down to business
To turn the world upside down

Gazing Globe

Hungry River courses the gorge
below the tiers of a warehouse
where fire-breathers mouth long tubes,
blowing life into glass.

In the bubbles churning the mill,
In the black New England water,
these shapes that sent us forward
might come to us as vague longing, now.

Not memory, but some insistence of figure,
trying to form across time
and within the images the mind
finds at a past place.

A kiss, a flick of the wrist,
and molten globs spin into bulbs,
then blooming tulip goblets.
A longer kiss blows open bowls.

Some thing never asked,
we never asked for.
Water, fire, lips—
desire took its form.

The river's name, we remember in our own light.
The glass, alive when we saw it, now frozen into vases,
not chalices, not orbs that might make sense
of this our backward gaze.

Goodnight

Goodnight. Why stay awake?

When Nanaboozho's been caught drinking,
down at the Tomahawk
with half-a-dozen of your cousins—
hard to tell who's which or what.

Those Roman soldiers about to get
their asses kicked 'cause
you're a great shot
at pool. Never happened before

you slept. No where else
can the glow of one cousin's name
feel like a real hand, held to your own,
but not quite met—
his smile lazy as you wept
and felt the better for it before

Roman legions bet
your army of dead cousins
the usual pool-hall, bar-room
threat and boast and gold

discs flare across
green felt in the glow of
Grainbelt mirrors
green dollars ugly money
but fair's fair to figments.

Nanaboozho takes the lucre and runs.

Ki yippee ki yi yaay!
Howah!
Hokah hey . . .

Ssssss . . . Don't wake anyone.

Recline on the red cape
of Marious or Giaus or Platypus,
any one of the muscled Romans who woo
you brutishly—but for the yanking geese

fresh from a Woodland School painter's sky
Morisseau's all-seeing eye of sun
must have sent them to wake you.

But no. You can resist the real.

Greasy oil-paint cormorant
Waterbird dives and surfaces
with that same old lover you long for.

This is not a flying dream. No wings
but fur and paws and earthy activities about to commence

when those same dead cousins pull up
in some old beater, actually a vacuum cleaner,
with a backseat, and you jump in 'cause
it's been so long since you went riding
with your cuz.

And the night swells sweet and plastered full
of green brush slapping as the boys drive, wild.

They crack the universe when they laugh,
bright energy shatters musically
into billions of fish flies across the pond-smooth
space-time expanse into which they've ditched.

Ditched you again. Just like when. Gone beyond.

On a good night you get
some of it back.

Goodnight. Why stay awake?

Post-Professorial

We learn, as we suspected, they're never done, the grades.
Though we color-code the folders, email, or post for days,
still there will be time for one last late paper, one revision
and extensions and revisions that a bad break up will unmake.
Our keys returned, our robes bagged and books boxed—
We learn, at last, that we never get the grades forever done.
The one tow-headed dude who stunned us with his delicate
diction or the cropped blonde whose political rants ran
red the day she showed up in ROTC uniform, will always
want us to take another look. Any door left ajar lets
in another draft.

We need some air here, anyway. Days beyond the classroom
where windows opened to allow flight, yes, but light
and fire which we swore students made in their own hands.
Remember that burning? Even a bit like love by mid-semester,
elemental, rare, natural—even, we learn, exhaustible.

A Plane Full of Poets

How often does that happen?
Stalled out like syntax, attacked
in perfect blue, or in first thunder.
We fasten our seat belts, wonder
out our round windows who's left
on earth to write for us,
elegize properly, or poorly,
the whole plane-load, should we go
down, ground, ditch
our diction, die mid-iamb.

Earthbound

Nothing out in space
beats nothing here
where tugs of blood
run our lungs and shallow
as breathe the echoed threat
this might be it.

She wraps and snatches
holds a shawl around
poor body, dumb-lucky
falling blankly.

World of glitter, all we want,
all we get.

World of water,
more than we all deserve, maybe.

Wise Solomon said
we all fall
upon the kindred earth,
our birth-cries common to all.

Yes, the earth is kin
and kind and red.

World of dust, clay, mud—
All we make, in the end.

She sometimes steps
on a crack, taps it open,
hopes it swallows her whole.

Other times she stares
light beams beyond,
bodily gone to the sky.

Yet even those few shuttle
crew who broke gravity
can't escape
earthliness,
the downward trend
obsession's pull,
a human urge for dirt.

Earthbound.
It's trying to get up
that gets us down.

After Words

Is that all there is?
—Peggy Lee

He's a brilliant playwright,
with attendant torment
and so he'd like to end with:
That's the way I like it—
A little KC Sunshine B. for epitaph.

For another friend
it all depends on when.
Last spring it might have been:
It's all a mystery.
Last fall it might have been Pink Floyd
I'll see you on the dark side of the moon—
This year, it would probably be:
Now it's dark.

One of my sisters would leave us with
Wait a sec, this is just the rough draft . . .
While the other two remain silent as the grave
when asked what they'd like inscribed.

My poet friend favors Bishop's question of travel:
Should we have stayed at home, / wherever that may be?
Ballerina Sally has it easy:
Dancing on my Grave, from Gelsey Kirkland

But what could lawyer Anne mean?
Oops, I did it again
Surely she won't let pop divas bleat her last words?

Someone answered my emailed query with
DEEP, DEEPER, DEEPEST
Sounds right for the fine and private place.

But, really, scatter my ashes, baby—
from said playwright, about says it,
for after words.

Author's Note

Again and again, Kennewick man and other similar human remains used for osteological study are referred to as "national treasures" and a source from which to gather invaluable information and data to reconstruct the lives and migrations of the "first Americans," for the benefit of all Americans.

At what point does a body become common property, and who in reality is this "common humanity" to which they refer? Is it really "all Americans" that are interested in and feel they would benefit from knowing about Kennewick man? If Kennewick man is envisioned as a treasure trove of ancient wisdom, one must ask what this information might be, and why do those persons who argue most vehemently in favor of scientific study feel it to be so vastly important? Why the insistence on overlooking ethnic and cultural distinctions, agendas, and definitions and the repeated argument that Kennewick man belongs to "all of us," is "our ancestor," and is part of the history of "our homeland"?

—Suzanne J Crawford, "(Re)Constructing Bodies:
Semiotic Sovereignty and the Debate over Kennewick
Man," in *The Repatriation Reader*

* * *

Unearthed.

Nothing much stays buried in the dark. Not much left an e-search won't excavate. Rat-chewed nuts prove Maori tenure on New Zealand, and Toumai-sweet speckled skull of a human-chimp half-breed, these unearthed and brought to light on our computer screens.

Stable isotopes of DNA teased from mummies determine corn-fed children died fat and happy. Follow a link to the words of an Incan girl who said to a Spanish chronicler: *Finish with me now, because the celebrations they held for me in Cuzco were enough.*

Dig the internet and you'll find skullduggery abounds: Osceola's head, removed by an Army surgeon and embalmed, traveled north to wind up in the Surgical and Pathological Museum, burned to the ground in 1866—but stories of Osceola head trips persist.

Blackhawk, also beheaded, skull also lost to museum fire, might envy Geronimo whose head bones get kissed by Yale's Presidents-to-Be if we are to believe the boast of Skull and Bones—the Bush and Kerry secret sect—who seemed to believe the tale themselves, who offered Geronimo's descendants a skull whose toothy death's head smile turned out to belong to a ten-year-old child.

More wonderful to find 5,000-year-old gum dug up by students in Finland yields DNA. What we don't learn from quids mouthed millennia ago, we may well find in fossil feces, coprolites 14,300 years old pre-date Clovis and open land-tenure questions never dreamt of by an ancestor who kept his head, but dined on grouse then took relief in a cave one fine long, long ago day just now come to light once more.

✳   ✳   ✳

This collection of poems began first as response to monuments of literature that use indigenous figures as metaphor, but then as a consideration of scared spaces and the risks we humans pose to the landscape. I was curious about what places indigenous people would consider their national monuments. My poetic eye shifted quickly from endangered mountains to the body. The body itself is the place of monument and has been treated as such by science as well as religion across cultures.

Because the body has become a location, a site and a text to scholars, what would seem violation of a scared space (say a temple or shrine) becomes a legitimatized and urgent need of study. The rules in place to protect our bodies when we die simply do not apply to anyone who has been dead long enough. That seeming contradiction troubles me and made me want to express my dis-ease learning that an ancestor's bones have been crushed for testing.

Accompanying my unease is a giddy and uncomfortably amused fascination with how we can now know what ancient people ate for their last meals. We can learn if relics of saints date correctly to the time the blessed person walked the earth. Famous skeletons and skulls get gender re-assigned regularly and miracles can be debunked in a lab, just like that!

Eventually, in writing these poems, I moved from the depersonalized study of the dead to my own thoughts on the body and on loss. Beginning and ending this collection are poems that touch on the fate of young American Indian men whose life expectancy is still very far below other ethnic groups. Part of my writing comes from that deepest of concerns.

∗　∗　∗

Returned.

A Tattooed Maori head gets returned. The Field Museum hosts ceremony given by Ojibwe for new Zealand kinsmen. Bushels of bones from the Smithsonian go home. And in Australia, police receive skulls from Freemasons who say they're Aborigine, once used in Masonic ritual. Many treasures looted from Baghdad make miraculous return. American bodies ship out daily from Iraq. Thousand and thousands of bones come home. And in Iraq, thousands of bodies of that earth go back.

∗　∗　∗

Notes to National Monuments

"Guidelines for the Treatment of Sacred Objects" slightly spoofs the Native American Graves Protection and Repatriation Act, Public Law 101-601.

"Mahto Paha, Bear Butte" considered sacred to several tribes, the area of the Black Hills of South Dakota is the scene of an intense battle between Native people and other groups, including Christian motorcycle groups, who wish to put up churches there.

"Grand Portage" is one of two National Monuments in my home state of Minnesota.

"Some Elsie": All the Elsie poems refer to William Carlos William's poem "To Elsie."

"Made in Toyland" was written before the lead-tainted toys scare of 2007–2008.

"Ghost Keeper": The title and the quote are from *The Shadow or Ghost Lodge: A Ceremony of the Oglala Sioux*, by Alice Fletcher.

"*De'an*": This poem came about after noticing Meg Noori use the Ojibwe word *Ode'an*.

"The Lone Reader and Tonchee Fistfight in Pages" refers to a title by Sherman Alexie.

"Star Blanket Stories" refers to indigenous star myths and stories about star quilts.

"Body Works" does not refer to the show of this title, but another much like it.

"eBay Bones": Such an auction took place. Multiple internet sources cite the event.

"My Beloved Is Mine" uses language from Shakespeare's *The Tempest*.

"Kennewick Man Tells All" and all the poems in the Kennewick Man series were influenced by an essay by Susan J. Crawford in *Repatriation Reader: Who Owns American Indian Remains?*

"Prisoner No. 280" refers to the French Queen, Marie Antoinette.

"Girl of Lightning" contains a complex set of responses to readings about the display of child mummies in South America. A discussion board on the subject posted by *American Renaissance* prompted outrageously racist responses. The discussion posts have since been taken down.

Please see the author's website *HeidErdrich.com* for more sources and discussion of these poems and other events mentioned in her author's statement.